THE
ROBOT
BOOK

Author: Sarah Chapman
Consultants: Dr. Jim Wyatt,
Dr. Mark Gasson, Isaac Ashdown
Illustrator: Jamie Oliver
Editor: Emily Hawkins
Design: Ali Scrivens, Mo Choy
Picture Editor: Frances Vargo
Paper Engineer: Liza Lau
Art Director: Miranda Kennedy
Production Director: Clive Sparling

First edition for the United States and Canada
published in 2006 by Barron's Educational Series, Inc.
© 2006 Andromeda Children's Books
An imprint of Pinwheel Ltd
Created and produced by
Andromeda Children's Books,
an imprint of Pinwheel Ltd
Winchester House, 259–269 Old Marylebone Road,
London, NW1 5XJ, UK

All inquires should be addressed to:
Barron's Educational Series, Inc.
250 Wireless Blvd.
Hauppauge, NY 11788
www.barronseduc.com

ISBN-13: 978-0-7641-7964-8
ISBN-10: 0-7641-7964-0

Library of Congress Control No.
2006920215

Printed in China

9 8 7 6 5 4 3 2 1

PICTURE CREDITS

L = left   R = right   T = top   B = bottom
5L Courtesy of Honda, 5BR Corbis/Louis Psihoyos,
7B SPL/James King-Holmes, 8R SPL/Peter Menzel,
9T SPL/Spencer Grant, 10B Rex Features/Sipa Press,
11T SPL/David Parker, 12 Courtesy of Carnegie Mellon & NASA,
13R Rex Features/Action Press, 14 NASA, 15 Courtesy of JAXA
Hyabusa, 16B NASA, 17T NASA, 18L Rex Features/Intuitive
Surgical, 19B SPL/Sam Ogden, 20R Courtesy of iRobot,
21T Courtesy of NEC Corporation, 21B Courtesy of Toshiba
Corporation, 22 Hasbro UK, 23B Courtesy of Sony,
24 Lucasfilm/20th Century Fox/The Kobal Collection/Keith
Hamshere, 25L 20th Century Fox/CBS Television/The Kobal
Collection, 25R Courtesy of Honda, 26B SPL/Peter Menzel,
27R SPL/Roger Harris, 28T SPL/James King-Holmes,
29 SPL/Peter Menzel, 30 SPL/Eurelios/Delphine Aures,
31 SPL/Mauro Fermariello

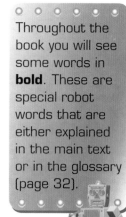

Throughout the
book you will see
some words in
bold. These are
special robot
words that are
either explained
in the main text
or in the glossary
(page 32).

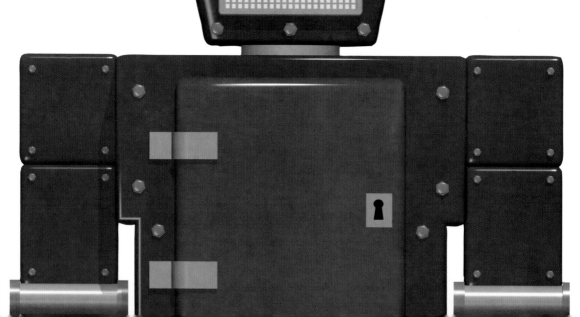

Contents

WHAT IS A ROBOT?

Robots are everywhere! You can define a robot as any machine that works automatically and does a job that human beings want it to do. We have made robots that will do things that we can't do, such as exploring the surface of Mars, or don't want to do, such as housework.

POWERING UP

To work, the first thing a robot needs is a power supply. This is often a battery, so that the robot can move without a power lead. A robot also needs a **central controller**, which is its "brain." This lets the robot "think" for itself, within the limits set by the program.

AT YOUR SERVICE

Robots are designed to help us. They do routine jobs in factories, or work in dangerous places, discovering things and improving our knowledge. Sometimes, people feel more comfortable with robots that look and behave like humans, rather than machines. These robots are called **androids** or **humanoids**.

Hi, I am Rusty

I am your personal security guard, at your service. Just like all robots, I need four things in order to function:

1. A way of gathering information, like a sensor.

2. A way of performing a task, like arms or legs.

3. A central controller, linking 1 and 2 together.

4. A power source, such as a battery.

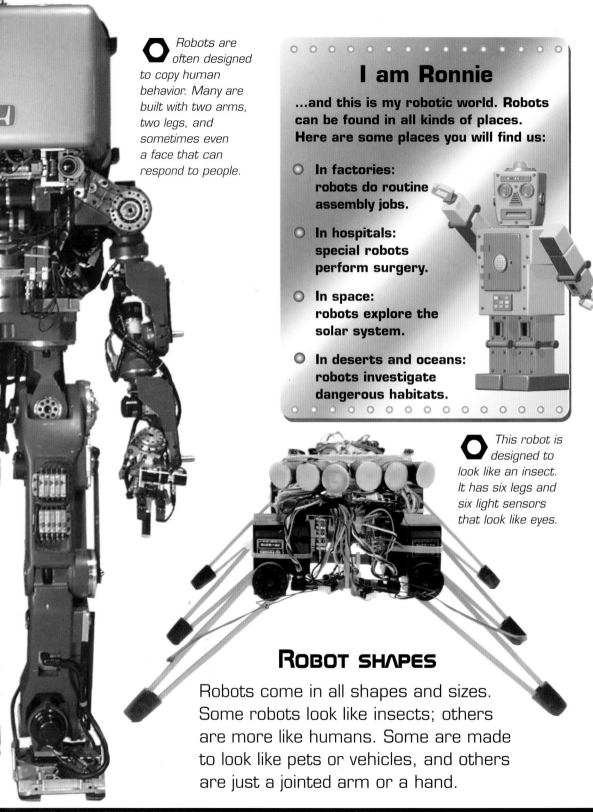

Robots are often designed to copy human behavior. Many are built with two arms, two legs, and sometimes even a face that can respond to people.

I am Ronnie

...and this is my robotic world. Robots can be found in all kinds of places. Here are some places you will find us:

- **In factories:** robots do routine assembly jobs.

- **In hospitals:** special robots perform surgery.

- **In space:** robots explore the solar system.

- **In deserts and oceans:** robots investigate dangerous habitats.

This robot is designed to look like an insect. It has six legs and six light sensors that look like eyes.

ROBOT SHAPES

Robots come in all shapes and sizes. Some robots look like insects; others are more like humans. Some are made to look like pets or vehicles, and others are just a jointed arm or a hand.

How Do Robots Work?

All robots work by gathering information, processing it, then doing something in response to that information. You could say that there are three stages that work in a continuous process: the input, process, and output.

The three stages

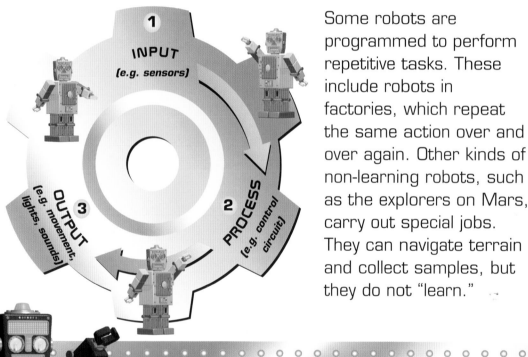

1 INPUT *(e.g. sensors)*

2 PROCESS *(e.g. control circuit)*

3 OUTPUT *(e.g. movement, lights, sounds)*

Non-learning robots

Some robots are programmed to perform repetitive tasks. These include robots in factories, which repeat the same action over and over again. Other kinds of non-learning robots, such as the explorers on Mars, carry out special jobs. They can navigate terrain and collect samples, but they do not "learn."

Robot hardware

The hardware of a robot is everything we robots are made of. Different robots need different kinds of hardware. This hardware includes:

- Lights, sounds, or motorized parts.

- A power source, such as a battery.

- The electronics that contain our program.

- Our sensors.

THE WORD "ROBOT" WAS FIRST USED IN A CZECH PLAY IN THE 1920s

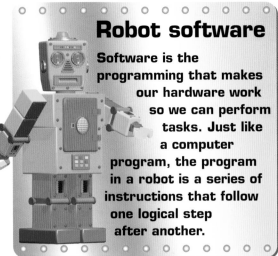

Robot software

Software is the programming that makes our hardware work so we can perform tasks. Just like a computer program, the program in a robot is a series of instructions that follow one logical step after another.

LEARNING ROBOTS

Robots can also be programmed to learn from the information they gather. For example, scientists have developed a group of small, wheeled robots that recognize objects and decide whether to move toward or away from them. Gradually, they learn to vary the decisions they make.

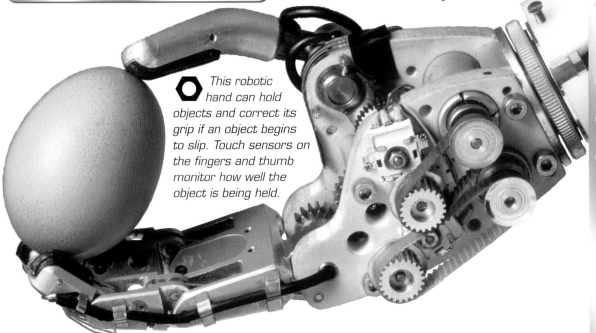

This robotic hand can hold objects and correct its grip if an object begins to slip. Touch sensors on the fingers and thumb monitor how well the object is being held.

BIO-INSPIRED ROBOTS

In order to get a robot to perform a task, it is useful for scientists to understand how a human or animal would do it. To design robotic hands that work like human ones, robot makers study how our hands grip and turn, and how they react to holding different objects. Scientists copy nature to design robots that move like animals, such as spiders, snakes, and cockroaches.

WHAT CAN ROBOTS DO?

Robots can do many things that once only humans or animals could do. Most people do not realize that some robots can understand their surroundings, plan their actions, and learn new things. Robots can be programmed to carry out all kinds of jobs in many different fields, from medicine to transport and from industry to recreation.

WALKING, CLIMBING, CRAWLING

It is hard to build a robot that can walk on two legs like us, so robot makers often use wheels or caterpillar tracks to allow robots to move around. These make the robots stable, so they are able to move on uneven surfaces without falling over. Some robot makers copy insects and design robots with six legs. These robots are much more stable than robots with just two legs. Each insect leg has its own motor and moves independently.

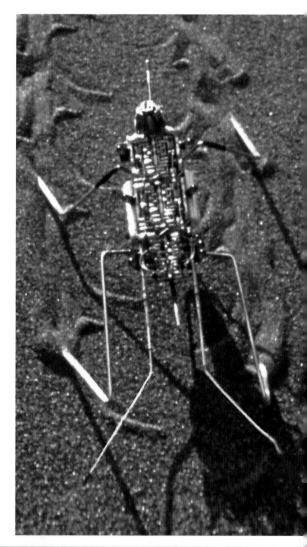

⬡ *The legs of this robot insect are suited to walking through sand dunes. This robot learns about its environment as it goes. Scientists hope that robots like this could eventually be used to clear land mines.*

Fetching and Carrying

Some robots, usually called **grippers**, use jaws and scoops to collect and fetch things. For example, some robots collect ore from mines deep underground that are too dangerous for humans. Jaws and pincers can also be used to move dangerous items, such as unexploded bombs, out of harm's way.

We can carry dangerous items!

A bomb disposal robot picks up a bomb using its robotic claw.

Robots large and small

Nowadays, scientists can build all kinds of robots, from gigantic, super-powerful machines capable of doing heavy manual work, right down to the most delicate robots that carry out precise tasks. We robots can carry out delicate work much more precisely than humans.

Making Things

Robots are used to make all kinds of machines, such as cars and washing machines. They have replaced human workers in many factories, where they assemble components and weld them together. "Thinking" robots at a car manufacturer have made history as the first robots of their kind to have "eyes" and "brains" that allow them to complete tasks faster and more accurately than any human.

Robots in Factories

Industrial robots have taken over the dull and dangerous factory jobs that used to be carried out by humans. They never complain about physical problems and they do not need vacations. Many industrial robots work **24** hours a day, every single day of the year, and the production line never stops.

Robots on the Assembly Line

In factories such as car manufacturing plants, robots work tirelessly on many different tasks. They manipulate tools with their powerful arms, cutting and welding parts together with perfect precision. They repeat this process on each car body, never breaking into a sweat despite the heat. Farther down the line, more robots carry out the next task required, such as fixing screws and painting. Although humans no longer build most cars, a human technician has to monitor the working of the robots, repair them if necessary, and stop the production line if something goes wrong.

Robots like these, working on the production line for the VW Golf V, now carry out almost every aspect of car production.

NOWADAYS, MOST CARS ARE PRODUCED BY ROBOTS.

ROBOTIC ARMS

Robotic arms can be big, like those in car factories, but they can also be very small. Tiny robotic arms can make small items, such as batteries. They can even work at the microscopic level in laboratories, where safety precautions are very strict and contamination must be avoided. It is easier to make sure that conditions are sterile with robots, which never leave the building.

A robotic arm welding in a car factory. Robots are perfectly suited for these dangerous precision tasks.

Why use robots?

We robots can do all kinds of tasks in industry, from transporting materials to painting machine parts to assembling electronic circuits.

We don't get tired or become distracted, so we can carry out complicated tasks faster, more efficiently, and with fewer mistakes than humans.

ROBOTS FACING DANGER

Robots are lifesavers because they can do jobs in places that are far too dangerous for humans. They have been sent to work deep underground, at the bottom of the ocean, and even inside active volcanoes. They can also deal with emergencies, such as finding and defusing bombs, and putting out fires.

HEAT AND DUST

Robots that can tackle difficult landscapes have been sent to gather information from remote areas such as deserts, polar regions, and active volcanoes. In 1994 the eight-legged **Dante II** robot explored the crater of Mount Spurr, a volcano in Alaska. It took samples of water and gases released by the volcano, and recorded video images.

⬡ *Dante II inside the crater of active volcano Mount Spurr. Missions like this show that robots can work in harsh environments— they have even been used to explore other planets.*

.....SOME ROBOT SUBMARINES CAN DIVE TO A DEPTH OF 19,700 FEET (6,000 M).................

Emergency service

Robots have been designed to fight fires, especially in hazardous areas like chemical plants or nuclear reactors. Built to cope with the heat of an inferno, **robotic firefighters** go right into the fire and remove flammable or dangerous chemicals. These robots can see what is happening inside the blaze with cameras that beam back video pictures. People can assess the fire and control the robots from a safe distance.

Underwater explorers

The UK's Met Office (a provider of environmental and weather-related services) will soon have 3,000 robot submarines patrolling the world's oceans. Robots in the ARGO Program (Array for Real-time Geostrophic Oceanography) monitor the temperature of the oceans to improve forecasting and our understanding of climate change. Each six-foot-long ARGO weighs about 66 pounds (30 kg), and drifts between 3,300 and 6,600 feet beneath the waves.

Bomb disposal

Bomb disposal units rely on robots to take on the dangerous task of finding and defusing bombs. These robots are built to withstand the shock of an explosion.

⬡ *This firefighting robot directs its extinguisher into the center of a fire. An extinguisher may contain water, foam, powder, or gas, depending on the type of fire.*

Under the ocean

Robot submarines can reach the bottom of some of the deepest oceans, where humans cannot go. Controlled from a support ship by a special connecting line, a robot submarine can recover torpedoes, collect samples, and explore.

ROBOTS IN SPACE

With their ability to carry out tasks in the most hostile environments, robots have been vital to space exploration. They have traveled toward the Sun and to the farthest reaches of the solar system to help us uncover its deepest secrets. Robots in orbiting satellites can also help us understand our own Earth.

SATELLITES AND SPACE STATIONS

Many types of unmanned satellites orbit the Earth. They include research satellites like the **Hubble Space Telescope**, weather satellites, and satellites for communication and navigation. They all gather information and send it back to earth. Manned space stations also orbit the earth. The **International Space Station** (ISS) is the latest one, still under construction in space. More than 100 components are being assembled by humans and robots. The robotic arm of the International Space Station enables the astronauts to move around in space. The arm has three human-like joints (a shoulder, an elbow, and a wrist) and also a hand. Soon a smaller, two-armed robot will perform the delicate assembly tasks that are currently handled by astronauts during spacewalks.

In 2005, an astronaut used the ISS robotic arm to make the first in-flight repairs to a space shuttle.

...SPACE PROBES CAN TAKE PHOTOS OF ASTEROIDS SO CLOSE-UP THAT PEBBLES ARE VISIBL

Space probes

We have gained new insights into the nature of space through probes that have **intelligent systems** on board. Scientists have learned a lot about the Sun with the **SOHO** (Solar and Heliospheric Observatory) space probe. Expected to last just two years when launched in 1995, it continues to send a stream of information back to Earth. From it, we are learning how the Sun works and how to predict the impact of its activity on Earth. The **NEAR** (Near Earth Asteroid Rendezvous) **Shoemaker** robot explorer returned data about the

The Hayabusa probe, which touched down on the Itokawa asteroid in 2005.

asteroid Mathilde as it flew by it in 1997. The explorer landed on the surface of the asteroid Eros in 2001. It sent back pictures of a place where no machine, let alone any human, had gone before.
A Japanese probe has become the first craft to collect samples from the surface of an asteroid. The **Hayabusa** ("falcon") briefly touched down on the Itokawa asteroid in December 2005 and fired a projectile to loosen surface material. Scientists believe it collected the debris, but will only be sure when it returns in 2007.

VOYAGES OF DISCOVERY

We have sent robots on voyages to several planets in the solar system, including far away Uranus and Neptune. But the planet about which we have discovered the most is Mars, thanks to two little robot rovers that are still hard at work on the red planet.

ROVERS ON MARS

After a year-long journey, in January 2004 two powerful robots landed on Mars. Right away these twin explorers, **Spirit** and **Opportunity**, began taking and sending back 360-degree pictures. Then they drove off to begin exploration. These robots are programmed to follow a plan while adapting to unexpected changes in their environment. In the course of their tireless fieldwork, they have sent back over 70,000 images and helped us gain a new understanding of Mars. The rovers were designed to last only 90 sols (Martian days) until April 2004, but were still going strong at the end of 2005—seven times their expected lifetime. In this time they have traveled over three miles (5 km).

Using information the rovers send back to Earth, scientists tell them where to go next to analyze different rocks and soils in order to find out if there was once water on Mars.

Galileo

One of the most successful voyages of planetary exploration was the Galileo spacecraft's mission to Jupiter. Launched in 1989, Galileo reached our solar system's biggest planet in 1995 after a journey of nearly 3 billion miles (5 billion km). It circled Jupiter 34 times, sending back 14,000 pictures and other data, before disintegrating in Jupiter's dense atmosphere in September 2003. It provided important information about Jupiter and its four largest moons.

The Galileo spacecraft spent eight years circling Jupiter and sending back information.

Mars rovers: the facts

○ Each of the robot rovers has six wheels and is the size of a golf cart.

○ Their instruments include a camera, an imager, spectrometers (which provide information about rocks on Mars), and a tool used to expose fresh rock surfaces for study.

○ They are powered by solar panels and rechargeable batteries.

○ They have been trained to recognize and move through difficult terrains.

○ They can travel up to 130 feet (40 m) in a Martian day.

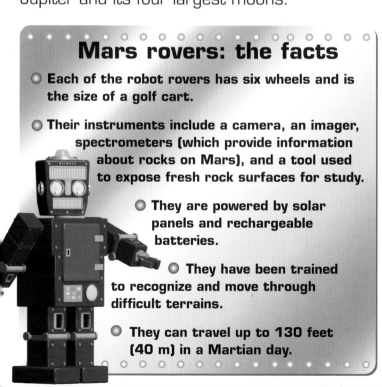

Cassini-Huygens

The largest interplanetary spacecraft ever built arrived at Saturn in July 2004 after a seven-year journey. The Cassini spacecraft will orbit Saturn for four years, surveying the planet and its moons. The Huygens probe is the first to touch down on land in the outer solar system—on the surface of Titan, Saturn's largest moon.

ROBOTS IN MEDICINE

Surgeons use robots to help them with their work. Specially designed robots can get to places in the human body that are difficult for hand-held instruments to reach. These robots can work more precisely than surgeons. They are used for a range of procedures, including heart surgery, removing tumors, and repairing arteries.

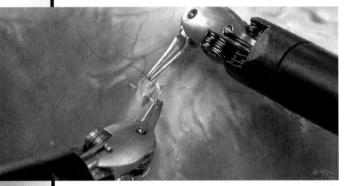

*The **da Vinci** is a robot used in operations, seen here performing heart surgery. The arms are thin enough to allow surgery through incisions only half an inch (1 cm) wide.*

IN THE OPERATING ROOM

Robots are often used to perform surgery. Cameras mounted on a robot's arms deliver images to a TV screen. A human surgeon follows the progress of the operation on the screen and controls the robot remotely, using joysticks to direct tools at the end of the robot's arms.

CYBER SURGERY

Another robot used in medicine is the **CyberKnife**. It is not a knife at all, but a radiation tool on a robotic arm that can remove tumors and lesions. The CyberKnife can do this without making an incision, and with no pain to the patient. This robot can find those tumors that nothing else can reach.

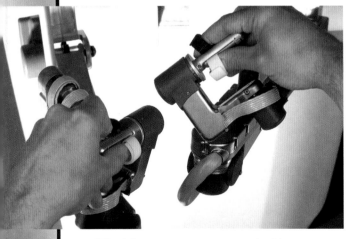

A human surgeon controls the da Vinci robot using joysticks.

SURGICAL ROBOTS HAVE MECHANICAL WRISTS THAT MOVE JUST LIKE HUMAN WRISTS..

Repairing blood vessels

Robots are being made smaller and smaller. Tiny robot tools can be inserted into veins and arteries to clear blockages from blood vessel walls that restrict blood from flowing properly.

Haptic helpers

Haptic means "touch." Haptic robots allow people to "feel" virtual objects (objects that are not really there). Some haptic robots can help patients, such as stroke victims, who need to exercise their sense of touch and develop movement. One of these robots is a virtual-reality device called a **PHANToM Haptic Interface**. It allows the user to "feel" the texture, temperature, shape, and weight of virtual three-dimensional objects with a pen-shaped tool or a thimble sensor worn on a fingertip. It may eventually be used in surgery.

Medical training

Humanoid robots can reproduce the symptoms of various diseases and conditions, providing realistic training for doctors. One simulates heart disease, one can "suffer" lung conditions, and a third is used in ear-nose-throat training.

We robots can help people who have limited movement.

⬡ *Haptic robots use the sense of touch in human interactions with a computer. This virtual-reality haptic device allows the user to "feel" and move a three-dimensional object shown on the screen.*

ROBOTS IN THE HOME

Would you like a robot that can turn on your TV, turn off your lights, check your messages, and do the housework? Scientists have developed robots that can do all this and more. One day, it is likely that we will all have a helpful little robot to look after us at home.

DOMESTIC SERVANTS

The day when robots perform household chores is getting closer with the arrival of robotic **vacuum cleaners** that clean floors at the touch of a button. These cleaners can learn the layout of a room and move around it precisely, cleaning thoroughly and recognizing when the job is done. They can even charge their own batteries!

◆ More than one and a half million homes have a **Roomba**®, which will vacuum your floors while you do something more fun. If it gets stuck you will hear it beep sadly, and when it has finished the job it will beep cheerfully, then drive itself onto its charger to recharge.

Robotic guard dogs

Some of the latest domestic robots are a bit like guard dogs. When you are away, your robot will look for intruders, record what it sees, and e-mail the recording to you as a video message.

"Can I help you?"

Imagine a walking, talking, seeing, hearing personal robot that makes itself a useful member of the household! **Wakamaru** and **PaPeRo** are cute, fun robots designed to make a difference in everyday life. They can recognize thousands of words and speak to and identify family members. They can move around the home, remembering each room, and turn your appliances on and off at your request. They can connect to the internet, let you know what your schedule is, tell you if you have e-mail, and even read it for you!

⬡ *PaPeRo is a friendly little robot that is simple to use. It will come to you when you call it and ask what it can do for you.*

Handy helpers

Toshiba's robotic companions **ApriAlpha** and **ApriAttenda** can carry out a variety of tasks. They can hold a simple conversation, control household appliances, read e-mail, and give news and weather updates. ApriAlpha, the smaller of the two, is also known as Apri Sharp Ear because it can distinguish different voices from any direction. It can talk to one person and then turn to respond to a question from another. ApriAttenda identifies its owner by the color and texture of his or her clothing. It will follow you around and stop when you do. If it cannot see you, it will call out for you.

⬡ *ApriAlpha (left) and ApriAttenda (right) are "life support partners" designed to help people, especially the elderly and young children, both in and out of the home.*

Can Robots Feel?

Robots are getting more intelligent all the time. You can buy robots that react to events and make decisions. Some even have complex, brainlike processors that develop as they gather information. Some have such expressive faces that you might think these lifelike robots must have feelings too.

Intelligent design

If robots are to share our everyday lives, they need to be able to understand and express feelings, or at least to appear to do so. You could almost believe that some robot toys, such as the **Furby**, are real creatures with feelings.

They mimic the way we humans show our emotions. Not only do they look like lovable pets, but the more you love and play with them, the more they will respond and "love" you back. We need to remember, though, that these robots have been programmed by humans. Designers like to give robots expressive faces and behaviors to make them more lovable.

⬡ *Furby can talk, giggle, and even "breathe"—moving its belly in and out. It dances, sings, tells jokes, and plays games, using hundreds of programmed words and phrases in "Furbish" and English.*

Furby can look happy, sad, and tired.

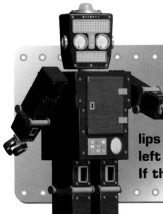

Humanoid toys

I am a humanoid robot. There are some humanoid robots with expressive faces. Their eyelids, eyes, and lips can move, showing a whole range of "emotions." When left alone they look sad, but when they see a face they smile. If their owner moves too fast, they can even look scared!

ROBOT PETS

There are many robot pets on the market. You can train some of the best robot dogs to sit, beg, jump, run, and shake paws. They have a range of moods, from playful to curious, angry, depressed, and even rude. If you are too nice to your pet it becomes naughty, and if you are mean, it will become shy.

⬡ The AIBO puppy shows you when it is "happy," "sad," "angry," or "surprised." It especially enjoys being petted under its chin.

The AIBO dog can interact with people!

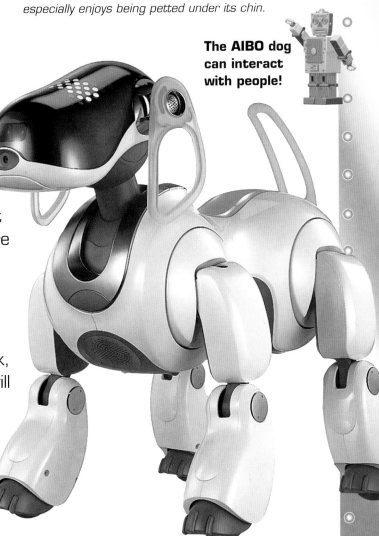

PUPPY PAL

Sony's **AIBO** puppy "learns" as it interacts with you. It can bark, fall over, get up, and sleep. It will recognize your face and voice, and respond to more than 100 words and phrases. People say that owning an AIBO is just like having a real dog.

Famous Robots

The most famous robots are usually from books, movies, and TV shows. Some are likable, gentle characters, while others turn against their creators. Some even have minds of their own and are, in some ways, superior to their human masters.

Movie robots

The entertainment industry has always been fascinated by robots. The first movie robot, the evil **Maria**, appeared in the 1926 film *Metropolis*, which was about technology running wild. The unnamed robot from *Lost in Space*, **Robbie the Robot** from the 1956 movie *Forbidden Planet*, and **R2D2** and **C-3PO** from *Star Wars*, are all friendly servants. But many fictional robots rebel against humans and put their own survival first. Among the most famous of these are the computer **Hal** in *2001: A Space Odyssey*, the robots in *I, Robot*, and the android replicants in *Blade Runner*.

R2D2 and C-3PO are an entertaining double act from the *Star Wars* movies. C-3PO is a fussy, worry-prone android, whose motto is "We're doomed." R2D2, famous for his bravery, does not speak but communicates by whistling, beeping, and warbling.

Famous Humanoids

Japanese scientists are working hard to make humanoid robots that can interact with humans. The most famous humanoid is **ASIMO**. It has a powerful computer system, sensors, motors, and advanced walking technology. Each direction of robot movement is called a **degree of freedom**. ASIMO has 26 degrees of freedom. It is designed to be useful and helpful to humans.

⬡ *ASIMO can move naturally, avoiding obstacles. It can walk up and down stairs, run, and even dance! ASIMO can reach knobs and switches, hand a person an object, and shake hands.*

ASIMO is so lifelike, you might think that there was a person inside!

⬡ *Known simply as "Robot," this character from the cult '60s TV series* Lost in Space *was a friendly, intelligent servant of the Robinson family. His most famous words were, "Warning! Warning!"*

Robbie the Robot

Isaac Asimov wrote a famous short story about Robbie the Robot, purchased as a babysitter for a little girl. Robbie is a best friend to the child, and more lovable than either parent. But the girl's mother thinks Robbie is dangerous, so she gets rid of him. Robbie eventually proves his loyalty by saving the little girl from danger. Asimov wanted to show that robots could be good companions and not evil mutants out to harm us.

Robots of the Future

Robot technology is advancing rapidly and in about 30 years' time, today's robots will look incredibly primitive. Some people think that the robots of the future will be able to carry out all the tasks, physical and mental, that humans can do. It is just a question of deciding what it is we want them to do next.

Friends or foes?

In his 1920 play about humanoid machines that turn against their creators, Czech playwright Karel Capek put forward two big ideas about robots. First, that robots are supposed to do the boring and difficult jobs that humans cannot do, or do not want to do. Second, that robots are potentially dangerous. Not everyone accepts these two ideas. In 1940, the science-fiction writer Isaac Asimov imagined robots caring for our children and being our friends.

Will the robots of the future be slaves, friends, or enemies?

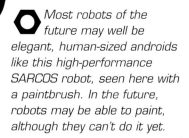

⬡ *Most robots of the future may well be elegant, human-sized androids like this high-performance SARCOS robot, seen here with a paintbrush. In the future, robots may be able to paint, although they can't do it yet.*

THE RISE OF THE ANDROID

Some of the world's most sophisticated robots are the **SARCOS** androids, constructed to be sensitive, good looking, graceful entertainers and party hosts. Scientists around the world are already developing more advanced sociable robots, which can recognize and express emotion and make good companions.

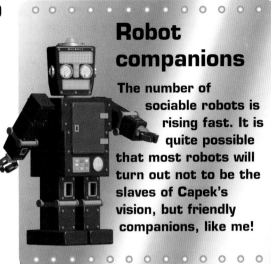

Robot companions

The number of sociable robots is rising fast. It is quite possible that most robots will turn out not to be the slaves of Capek's vision, but friendly companions, like me!

ROBOTIC ASTRONAUTS

NASA is developing the **Robonaut**—a humanoid robot with stereo-vision camera eyes and a jet pack. The Robonaut will copy the actions of a human operator who will guide it in its task. If developed and used on space stations, the Robonaut could take action whenever a problem needs fixing.

Nanorobots containing drugs will use propellers to move along the bloodstream to the target site, where they will inject the drug with their needle tip.

MICROSCOPIC ROBOTS

Microscopic robot technology (**nanotechnology**) could be developed in the future to treat diseases in new ways. For example, **nanorobots** might be used inside the body to clear blood clots or mend wounds.

They could even be implanted in the brain to improve our thinking skills. These new medical uses might also include the delivery of drugs and other substances to specific areas within the body.

CYBORGS

Part human, part machine, the cyborgs of science fiction have bodies crammed with electronic gadgetry that is wired to their brains. But what was once fiction is quickly becoming a reality that is within the grasp of scientists in the twenty-first century.

THE FIRST HUMAN CYBORG

Cyborgs are humans who have had their bodies "upgraded" with artificial organs or other body parts. Professor Kevin Warwick is the first human cyborg. He had a silicon chip **transponder** implanted in his arm. As he approaches his workplace at Reading University in England, a radio signal causes the chip to transmit a unique code identifying him. The doors of the building open, lights switch on, and his computer turns on. The chip allows people to keep track of his movements.

Professor Kevin Warwick holds a silicon chip transponder like the one that was implanted in his forearm in 1998, making him the first human cyborg.

What next for robots?

Our abilities are evolving rapidly. What might we be capable of in the future? We've come a long way since humans first thought of us. Humanoid robots could one day dominate the world. Cyborgs are not just science fiction!

.... SCIENTISTS ARE DEVELOPING COMPUTER CHIPS THAT CAN COMMUNICATE WITH NERVE

From science fiction to fact

A common theme in science fiction was that injured humans could be repaired using cyber-replacements for lost or damaged body parts. In medicine, such **artificial limbs** are a reality today. They are used to replace hands, arms, and legs lost in accidents. Wires and mechanical levers can be inserted into an arm to control a mechanical hand and allow it to grasp objects.

Mind over matter

Scientists believe that mind power could soon be used to control artificial limbs. **Microchips** implanted in the brain of paralyzed patients could allow them to control a robotic arm or leg. The electrical signals produced by the brain would be picked up by the chip and sent to the robotic arm. Advances in technology are transforming the design of artificial arms and legs, giving wearers a freedom of movement that would have been impossible a few years ago. Additions to the human body are doing everything but grow themselves, and scientists are even working on that too.

⬡ *A robotic hand with five jointed fingers mimics a human hand. Sensors on the wearer's skin detect electrical activity in the arm muscles. A built-in computer interprets the signals and orders the hand to open, close, or grip.*

A cyborg is a combination of human and machine!

WILL ROBOTS EVER TAKE OVER?

Even the most intelligent robots do not fully understand what we say to them—yet. But the gap between science fiction and science fact is closing fast, and some people are worried about what will happen if robots become as intelligent as humans. Will they turn against us?

ARTIFICIAL INTELLIGENCE

Some robot specialists believe that machines will never have human abilities, while others think that robots will take over the world. Some even think that people will become robots, as the consciousness of humans (*Homo sapiens*) merges with the bodies of robots, creating **Robo sapiens**. Engineers across the world are developing forms of artificial intelligence that are similar to human thinking processes. Robots will be controlled by "brains," or **neural networks**. Neural networks are programming systems based on the way the human brain works—robots may one day "think" like humans. Robots with neural networks start out with no knowledge and learn from their actions and experiences, just like humans.

⬡ *These evolving robots learn and develop. Over time, their programming adapts to their environment. If a robot manages to reach the light (on the left) twice in a row, it is called "evolved" and it may guide the other robots in the group to the light.*

Evolving robots

Scientists have developed groups of light-sensing robots showing "evolution" within their group. While their human makers want them to move to the light, the robots have not actually been given these instructions, so they have to "evolve," or develop, this behavior. **Evobots** are robots that use neural networks to learn and adapt to changing environments. They can also reproduce (in software and hardware) in a manner that imitates living things. Evobots can even be trained to play hockey.

⬡ The Robocup is an annual event where robots play soccer against each other. They have to run in different directions and kick a ball, and they need a high level of artificial intelligence. The competition aims to develop a team of robots that can beat the world's best human team by the year 2050.

How do we stop them?

How do we avoid the nightmare scenario of a battle between humans and robots? Isaac Asimov suggested that we could make sure robots do not become dangerous by programming them to follow these laws:

1. A robot may not injure a human being or allow harm to come to a human being.

2. A robot must obey orders from human beings, except where such orders conflict with the first law.

3. A robot must protect its own existence so long as this protection does not conflict with the first or second laws.

Glossary

Android Computer-controlled device in human form that can automatically perform certain actions in response to instructions; a humanoid

Artificial intelligence The ability of computer programs to mimic human thought processes

Central controller The "brain" of the robot, which processes information from its sensors and triggers its outputs

Circuit board A card or panel with a printed metal pattern and other components, forming a collection of integrated electrical circuits (chips)

Cyborg A human fitted with artificial organs or other body parts

Haptic Relating to the sense of touch

Humanoid A robot that looks and behaves like a human being

Intelligent Systems Computer programs that allow robots to learn from their surroundings and make decisions based on what they learn

Interface The point of connection between two computers, or between a computer and a user

Imager An instrument that makes an image using visible and infrared light

Microchip/silicon chip/chip A very small silicon object containing microscopic circuitry (usually called an integrated circuit) made to run computer programs

Neural network Programming system based on the way a human brain works

Processor/microprocessor A chip containing everything needed to make calculations and carry out instructions—the "brain" of a computer

Sensor Part of a robot that is used to detect and respond to information from its surroundings

Spectrometer A special camera used to measure the wavelengths of light given off by different types of rock

Transponder Electrical device that receives and responds to a signal

Virtual reality Interaction with computer-simulated events or environments

Index